SCIENCE PATROL

AT THE POLES

Louise and Richard Spilsbury

Gareth Stevens
PUBLISHING

Please visit our website, www.garethstevens.com.
For a free color catalog of all our high-quality books,
call toll free 1-800-542-2595 or fax 1-877-542-2596.

Cataloging-in-Publication Data

Names: Spilsbury, Louise.
Title: At the poles / Louise and Richard Spilsbury.
Description: New York : Gareth Stevens, 2017. | Series: Science on patrol | Includes index.
Identifiers: ISBN 9781482459685 (pbk.) | ISBN 9781482459708 (library bound) | ISBN 9781482459692 (6 pack)
Subjects: LCSH: Polar regions--Juvenile literature.
Classification: LCC G590.S65 2017 | DDC 578.0911--dc23

First Edition

Published in 2017 by
Gareth Stevens Publishing
111 East 14th Street, Suite 349
New York, NY 10003

Produced for Gareth Stevens by Calcium
Editors: Sarah Eason and Jennifer Sanderson
Designers: Paul Myerscough and Simon Borrough
Picture researcher: Rachel Blount

Picture credits: Cover: Shutterstock: Marcel Clemens (tl), fivepointsix (b), Incredible Arctic (tr), Armin Rose (cr), Jan Martin Will (cl); Inside: NASA: GSFC 41t, 41b; National Science Foundation: 26, 27t, Brian Barnett 25, Bob DeValentino 24, Jeffrey Donenfeld 23, Jennifer Heldmann 34, Lora Koenig 3, 28, Peter Rejcek 1, 20, 21, 29, 31, 33, 44, Mark Sabbatini 43, Kappa Pi Sigma U.S. Merchant Marine 18, Emily Stone 35, Emily Walker 32; NOAA: 37; Shutterstock: ArtTomCat 40, Tewan Banditrukkanka 19, Wim Claes 12, Drop of Light 42, FotoMonkey 8, Incredible Arctic 6, Kkaplin 11, Asmus Koefo ed 9, Kjetil Kolbjornsrud 13, Rich Lindie 36, Andy Morehouse 15, MP cz 7, Outdoorsman 14, Peppersmint 27b, Armin Rose 22, Yakovlev Sergey 5, I. Noyan Yilmaz 4, 30; Wikimedia Commons: DoD photo by Cmdr. Vincent Clifton, U.S. Navy 16–17, NASA 17, NASA/Jim Yungel 10–11, Brennanphillips 39, Felix Riess 45.

Printed in the China

CPSIA compliance information: Batch #CW17GS: For further information contact Gareth Stevens, New York, New York at 1-800-542-2595.

Contents

Chapter 1 Working at the Poles 4
Challenges and Changes 6
Daily Dangers 8

Chapter 2 Why Study the Poles? 10
Polar Resources 12
Climate Change and the Poles 14

Chapter 3 Lab Life 16
Food Supplies 18
Caring for the Environment 20
In the Lab 22

Chapter 4 Out and About 24
Survival in the Field 26
Shelter and Safety 28
Research Ships 30

Chapter 5 Cutting-Edge Technology 32
Ice Cores 34
Animal Studies 36
Robots at the Poles 38

Chapter 6 Amazing Discoveries 40
Discoveries that Help 42
Patrolling the Future 44

Glossary 46
For More Information 47
Index 48

working at the poles

Scientists who live and work at Earth's frozen poles have to cope with one of the most challenging types of **habitat** on the planet. Antarctica at the South Pole and the Arctic at the North Pole are among the coldest, remotest, and loneliest places in the world.

The Antarctic Continent

Antarctica is a giant mass of land known as a continent. It is almost completely covered in ice and snow. There are mountains and giant, slow-moving rivers of ice called **glaciers**. There are also huge, flat, open areas of ground called **ice sheets**. These are covered in ice up to 2 miles (3.2 kilometers) thick. In winter, the surface of the ocean around Antarctica freezes over and is covered in ice, too. The few lakes found here are mainly frozen over and there are not many plants. Any plants at the Arctic grow mainly in areas of **tundra**. Tundra is frozen land that is covered in snow and ice for most of the year, but that has some flowering plants in summer, when the snow melts.

Antarctica, which covers the South Pole, is the coldest, windiest place on planet Earth.

4

The Arctic Ocean

The Arctic region includes the frozen Arctic Ocean around the North Pole and parts of the countries of the United States (Alaska), Canada, Finland, Greenland, Iceland, Norway, Russia, and Sweden. These areas surround the ocean and are often covered in ice, too. In winter, the ocean is almost completely frozen into sheets of **barren** ice. In summer, the outer edges of the ocean ice melts. On Arctic lands around this ocean, there are hills and mountains, rivers and lakes, and areas of tundra. These areas can have a lot of plants or hardly any at all. Some have conifer (pine tree) forest.

Polar Differences

There are several differences between the Arctic and Antarctic. While the Arctic is sea surrounded by land, the Antarctic is land surrounded by sea. The Arctic is freezing, but because seawater does not drop below 28.4° Fahrenheit (-2° Celsius), it is not as cold as Antarctica. The poles have opposite seasons. When it is winter in one, it is summer in the other. Antarctica has hardly any plants and trees, but the Arctic has areas of tundra and conifer forest. However, for scientists working at the poles, the challenges are much the same— the cold, the lack of resources, such as wood or electricity, and the distance from services such as hospitals in case something goes wrong.

The ice of the Arctic Ocean is at least 10 –13 feet (3 –4 meters) thick.

5

CHALLENGES and CHANGES

Scientists at the poles have buildings they can live and work in for some of the time, but when they are on patrol—working and collecting samples or **data** outdoors—they are at the mercy of the polar **climate**. This can be dangerous and even deadly.

One of the biggest challenges facing polar scientists is the extreme cold. Getting very cold can cause a life-threatening condition called **hypothermia**. This can happen when people are working outside in freezing conditions, and their body temperature drops below 95° Fahrenheit (35° Celsius). When hypothermia sets in, the body stops working properly and starts to shut down. People become tired and confused and may not realize they are sick before it is too late. If hypothermia is not identified and treated quickly, people can die.

In a polar winter, there are 24 hours of darkness a day.

Lands of the Midnight Sun

The North and South Pole are known as lands of the midnight sun because, during the summer, the sun never sets. Every summer, the poles get about five months of continuous daylight, and in winter, they have five months of night. During summer, although scientists working outdoors might feel cold, any skin left uncovered can be exposed to the sun for hours and days on end, and so can be badly sunburned. The effects of the sun at the poles are intensified because sunlight **reflects** off the white surface of the snow and ice.

SCIENCE PATROL SURVIVAL

When scientists come to work at the poles, they have to be prepared for a long stay because it takes a lot of effort to get there. Transport to and from the South Pole can be undertaken only during the summer. In winter, the ice makes it almost impossible for ships to travel there. Most scientists stay for only one summer, or for two summers and one winter, before going home.

Why do you think most scientists only work at the poles for one season and not for more than one winter? How do you think it might affect people to be so far away from their family, home, and regular life for a length of time? Give reasons for your answers.

Scientists keep their skin covered and use sunblock to avoid sunburn. To stop the sun from burning their eyes and causing snow blindness they also wear sunglasses or snow goggles.

DAILY DANGERS

Scientists working at the poles face many dangers, from snow **blizzards** that make it impossible to see, to wild animals that can attack without much warning. Over time, scientists have learned more about polar hazards and how to deal with them.

Scientists traveling across the ice face several dangers.

Changing Views

Finding the way in a polar landscape is challenging because there are few landmarks. Most of the time, scientists are surrounded by an endless view of flat, white surfaces of ice and snow, which makes it very easy to become lost. Another problem is that the weather at the poles can change suddenly. Scientists might set out on patrol in sunshine, only to find that strong winds arrive within minutes that can blow in a snowstorm and cause a blizzard, making it impossible to see farther than a few feet ahead of themselves.

Dangerous Animals

Animal attacks on scientists are rare, but they do happen. Most animals that live in the tundra, such as reindeer, lemmings, and Arctic hares, are harmless. Other animals may attack humans if they are startled or hungry, or if they think they need to protect their young. Arctic wolves can work in packs to attack, while polar bears are able to knock a person unconscious or kill them with one swipe from their huge, clawed paws.

SCIENCE PATROL SURVIVAL

In the late nineteenth and early twentieth centuries, explorers took great risks to reach the poles and carry out scientific studies. From 1910 to 1913, Captain Robert Falcon Scott led a British expedition to reach the South Pole and carry out scientific experiments there. The explorers learned a lot about polar travel, about the movement of ice, and the equipment needed to survive there. But the trip was also a reminder of the dangers of polar exploration. Scott and four other men who reached the Pole itself died on the return to the expedition base.

How do you think the lessons learned by these early scientists and explorers and the discoveries they made have helped the expeditions that have ventured to the poles since? Remember that before these early expeditions, no one had visited the remotest parts of these regions.

In the Antarctic, leopard seals can pose a threat. These fierce **predators** have been known to burst through the thin ice at the edge of an ice sheet. They can grab a person with their powerful jaws and long teeth, and try to drag them into the water to kill and eat them.

Polar bears mainly eat seals, walruses, or whales, but they sometimes attack humans, too.

CHAPTER 2
Why study the poles?

There is nowhere else on Earth quite like the poles. They might look like icy wildernesses, but the poles are home to a wide range of living things that are **adapted** to the unique conditions there. This is a major reason why scientists study the polar regions.

Polar Life

Scientists study the plants and animals at the poles to learn more about how they live and how they interact with each other and the **environment**. Polar land animals range from minute tardigrades (water bears) to polar bears that weigh 1 ton (0.9 tonne), but many more animals live in and around polar waters. Krill are shrimp that are the length of a paper clip. They gather in millions in polar waters where there is plenty of **plankton** for them to eat. Whales, penguins, sea lions, and other animals feed on krill or the fish that feed on them. In turn, they attract predators, including orcas, polar bears, and leopard seals.

Extreme Survival

The coldest temperature recorded on Earth, -128.6° Fahrenheit (-89.2° Celsius), was recorded in Antarctica. However, life survives there. Scientists are fascinated by the ways that animals are adapted to survive the extreme cold. Adaptations range from thick blubber (fat) on walruses and whales to the blood of the Arctic cod, which has **antifreeze** in it. On Arctic land, there are plant survivors, such as Arctic willow, which grows low to hunker down out of the wind and cold. Tiny living things, such as **bacteria** and tardigrades, can even survive being frozen solid and then thawing.

Scientists study penguins for many reasons. One is to learn why they waddle. It seems waddling is the most energy efficient way for penguins to move about on ice!

Distinctive Landscape

Scientists study the poles for their special geography, too. For example, Antarctica has many ice features, including ice sheets over its surface and floating **icebergs**. The poles may look like another world, but studying them helps scientists learn about what our universe is made from. At the poles, scientists hunt for meteorites (space rocks that fall to Earth) because they are easier to spot on the snow or ice than on other parts of Earth.

Mountains peaks can be seen through the ice cover on Thurston Island off western Antarctica.

POLAR RESOURCES

Scientists play a vital role in studying how people affect polar wildlife and the polar environment when they come to the poles to take samples of natural resources such as oil and fish.

Oil Rush

The growing population of the world demands energy from burning oil to power its vehicles and machines. Reserves of oil on land and from beneath shallow seas worldwide are running out, so oil companies are exploring for new reserves deep under the Arctic Ocean. Exploiting these reserves could increase global oil by one-tenth. It might also pay to improve the lives of people in Arctic countries. However, it poses a massive risk for polar life. Animals may stop **breeding** in places where people start drilling. Oil spilled in water or trapped under ice can suffocate and poison marine life, and also **pollute** coastlines.

Oil can stick to the feathers of birds so they cannot trap warm air. This means the cold water will chill birds to death.

SCIENCE PATROL SURVIVAL

No one country owns Antarctica, but 39 nations look after territories, or sections, of it after signing the Antarctic Treaty. The treaty allows them to conduct and share research while looking after the Antarctic environment. The treaty bans any military activity, oil drilling, and mining on the land and ice shelves.

In the future, if oil and minerals are running out, do you think that countries might try to exploit Antarctica's reserves, such as its coal? How might this change Antarctica? Will this put pressure on the terms of the treaty? Explain your answers.

Polar Food

At the poles, fishing ships target fish such as Patagonian toothfish, but overfishing makes such fish **endangered**. Fewer fish at the poles means less food for polar animals, such as seals. The long lines with hooks used to catch toothfish also trap and kill rare birds called albatrosses in search of a fish meal. Krill are also being fished in their millions to make products such as health supplements and food for fish farms.

The poles are a new frontier for the world's fishing fleets because many fish stocks in warmer waters are running out.

CLIMATE CHANGE AND THE POLES

One reason the poles are of great interest to scientists is because they are important places to study Earth's changing climate. They help researchers judge the impact of this change now and in the future.

Climate Clues

One reason scientists study at the poles is because they can find evidence of past climates. For example, evidence frozen in or beneath the thick ice has revealed that there were once tropical forests on Antarctica. The ice also holds clues in the form of bubbles of trapped gas that show what Earth's **atmosphere** was like in the past.

Global warming forces walruses to crowd together so they risk trampling each other and not finding enough food to go around.

Global Warming

For thousands of years, the Arctic Ocean has remained partly frozen through summer. Now, as a result of global warming, the ice sheets and shelves at the poles are melting. Global warming is a rise in Earth's average temperature. It is caused by **greenhouse gases** trapping the sun's heat energy in the atmosphere. These gases, such as **carbon dioxide**, are increasing because there are more people burning coal, oil, and gas to power machines and to make electricity. Global warming is believed to be causing stormier, wetter, and drier weather patterns in different parts of the world, called **climate change**.

Melting polar ice is releasing more water into the oceans. This causes a rise in sea level that could flood low-lying coastal communities and shorelines.

Polar Impacts

Scientists study the poles partly because these icy places are experiencing strong impacts of global warming. Polar sea ice helps regulate Earth's climate, because the white ice reflects more of the sun's heat back into space than dark water does. Melting ice means that the planet is absorbing more solar energy, increasing global warming. The lack of ice is also affecting animals. For example, walruses usually rest on the ice and then swim down to plow the Arctic Ocean floor for clams and other prey. With less ice, they are forced to crowd together on any part of coastline near feeding grounds.

CHAPTER 3

LAB LIFE

Scientists who work at the poles live in research stations. They do laboratory work using data that they collect in the field. The scientists and the cooks, technicians, and other staff who live and work in research stations are the only people who live in Antarctica.

Types of Stations

Polar stations vary in design and scale. The largest in Antarctica is the US research station base at McMurdo. Like other large Antarctic stations, McMurdo is a permanent base. It has scientists working in laboratories on site and it provides support for more remote stations and scientists on field trips. Large stations have dormitories to sleep in, kitchens and dining areas, recreation rooms, several laboratories, storage areas, and often an aquarium where scientists can study sea life. Large stations often have runways or harbors, so planes and ships can reach them.

Around 1,000 people live at McMurdo in the summer and 250 in the winter.

Halley VI is a research station with moveable ski legs. The skis make it possible for the base to be towed to new sites.

Some research laboratories in the Arctic are built on islands or on the coastlines of countries around the Arctic Ocean. However, the Arctic covers a vast area, so some stations are erected on large masses of floating ice. This allows scientists to work nearer to the North Pole. Even though these bases are built on floating ice, they can still consist of several buildings, with living areas as well as laboratories to house scientific equipment.

Station Solutions

Both types of stations face challenges. Those at the Antarctic coast and on Arctic ice masses can be carried in the wrong direction when ice melts or moves. Far inland in Antarctica, the ice never melts, so rising levels of snow and ice could bury a station. The solution is to use a moveable station. Halley VI has units with legs that can be jacked up, or raised higher, to keep the base above snow that builds up on the ground beneath it. Halley VI is made up of a number of units or pods that can be attached to and detached from each other. Each pod can be adapted for a different use, such as for bedrooms or laboratories, as required.

FOOD SUPPLIES

Food is vital at the poles. Early explorers and scientists soon learned that the risk of hypothermia increased if people did not eat enough. This is because the human body needs extra **calories** to burn to keep itself at a normal, healthy temperature. It also requires more energy to do things like walking and working in the cold at the poles.

Food Stores

There are hardly any plants and very few animals at the poles that can be eaten, so scientists working there rely on deliveries of food. Most supplies are foods that can be stored for a long time, so they are frozen, dried, or canned. Fresh vegetables and fruit are a rare treat. They are only available just after a supply ship or airplane has visited.

There are also some high-calorie **dehydrated** foods that scientists can mix with melted snow to make a meal. Such foods have to be light to carry, packed with calories, and unable to freeze in the cold air. They are often used by scientists when they are working away from the research station for a day or longer.

A year's worth of food is brought in by ship.

Some stations grow fresh vegetables using a hydroponic system. Hydroponic systems have no soil. The plants grow in water that has nutrients added to it to replace those in soil.

SCIENCE PATROL SURVIVAL

Staff at smaller research stations often take turns cooking for each other. They usually sit down to eat together at the same time. However, even in large research stations that have kitchen staff to prepare the food, groups of people eat together in dining rooms. There are also coffee bars and recreation rooms with gadgets, such as karaoke machines, where scientists and other workers can meet.

Bedrooms are often quite small at a research station, with no space for eating meals or spending too much time. This is partly because space is limited but also to encourage people to get together. Why do you think this is important in a place like an isolated base at the poles?

Caring for the Environment

The poles are fragile places, so scientists are careful to ensure that their research stations and their activities do not have a negative impact on the environment. That means doing things like taking any waste home and avoiding disturbing the wildlife.

Waste Disposal

Pollution and waste can damage both the environment and its wildlife, so any waste the stations produce is removed or disposed of carefully. Some waste is removed by ship, while other waste is burned in an **incinerator** before ships take away the ash. Bases also have systems to clean wastewater from bathrooms and kitchens. Meals on bases usually include leftovers from the previous day to avoid wasting anything. Everything that is thrown away must be shipped home—and that costs money.

Workers pack up waste in the Waste Barn at McMurdo.

Halting Invasions

In the past, either intentionally or accidentally, people have brought plants and animals to the poles that do not exist there naturally. These invader **species** have caused serious problems. In the Antarctic, for example, rats from whaling ships destroyed many ground-nesting birds that had not encountered this predator before. Research stations are careful not to introduce any kind of life that could impact the natural environment. When fresh food is delivered to a station, it is checked and thoroughly washed in a special building to remove even tiny nonnative species, such as bacteria and bugs. When visitors, staff, and scientists first arrive, they have to clean their shoes and have their clothing and bags inspected for seeds and soils.

At the McMurdo wastewater treatment plant, microorganisms break down sewage waste until the liquid can be safely released into the ocean.

Getting Water

At the poles, people mostly get the water they need for drinking, cooking, and rehydrating dried foods by melting ice and snow. One problem with this is that the process uses a lot of fuel or electricity, and using fuel can cause pollution. Also, Arctic ice is formed from seawater, so it is salty and unsafe to drink. At some research stations, the residents make freshwater from seawater by filtering it through special, low-energy machines. This removes the salt and other impurities that make seawater dangerous for people to drink.

In the LAB

The labs and spaces where scientists work at the poles vary greatly. Larger research stations have several rooms and labs with a range of high-tech computers and equipment. Smaller research stations may have much more basic equipment and struggle to get the electricity they need to power them.

Power Sources

Getting fuel to stations to provide the electricity needed for powering a lab and other machines is expensive and difficult. The other problem is that burning fuel, such as diesel, releases carbon dioxide into the atmosphere and causes harmful pollution. That is why research stations try to use **renewable** sources of energy where they can. Some produce cheaper and more environmentally friendly power using **wind turbines**. Other stations use the plentiful sunlight at the poles to work **solar power** systems.

Wind turbines use the force of the strong polar winds to power generators and supply electricity and heat.

Teaching Spaces

In the Antarctic, the larger and more accessible research stations also have spaces where scientists can give talks and presentations to the tourists who travel there to see the sights and wildlife of the region. This is vital because it helps the public understand how important scientific research at the poles is. It may encourage people to support the scientists' work and also **conservation** of the poles.

Take a Tour!

The laboratory at McMurdo Station consists of five pods with a total area of 46,500 square feet (4,320 square meters). Each pod is used for a different type of scientific research, such as biology, chemistry, earth science, and **meteorology**. There are computer rooms, rooms where sections of ice and rock are studied, an electronics workshop, and rooms with special microscopes. There are three aquariums with wet labs and running seawater, where scientists can study sea life without having to put on scuba gear and dive under the ice. The aquariums often have live specimens of animals, such as Antarctic cod, krill, sea snails, giant sea spiders, urchins, sponges, and starfish.

This is the communications center at the Amundsen-Scott South Pole Station.

CHAPTER 4

Out and About

Scientists arrive at polar research stations at the ends of Earth by airplane or by ship. Once they are there, they also use a variety of motor vehicles to head out from their base to collect data and to carry out research in the field.

↑ This Sno-Cat is loaded with goods to transport.

Snowmobiles

Snowmobiles are small vehicles for one or two people that look like sleds with engines. They are simple to operate as they just have a accelerator and a brake. They are mainly used to get around, although they can also tow specialist scientific equipment on sleds. Snowmobiles have rubber tracks to grip slippery surfaces, with skis at the front to steer. Snowmobiles can travel at up to 50 miles per hour (80 kilometers per hour) on smooth snow and ice. In the Antarctic, people are not allowed to use dog sleds in case the dogs pass on diseases, such as **distemper**, to the seals.

Sno-Cats

Polar teams also need bigger, tougher vehicles that can haul equipment and supplies across the ice. Sno-Cats with caterpillar tracks can tow large sledges carrying supplies weighing up to 8 tons (7.2 tonnes). They have four separate, wide caterpillar tracks for gripping and staying stable on slippery or unstable ice. Sno-Cats can also be fitted with a snowplow so that they can be used to clear snow piles.

Rubber boots like these have thick rubber soles to help keep feet dry and grip snow and ice.

Thin Ice

Traveling around safely in the polar environment is not just about using motorized vehicles. Scientists need shoes with good grip and a wide sole so they do not sink into snow. They also need to learn about different kinds of ice. For example, dark or black colored ice is recently formed and usually thin. This makes it dangerous to stand on, because it is not strong enough to hold much weight. People can easily fall through it. It is safer to walk on white ice because this is usually at least 6 to 12 inches (15 to 30 centimeters) thick.

Survival in the Field

For scientists working on the ice, survival depends on wearing the right clothing for the icy conditions. Without it, scientists could find themselves in trouble. In the Antarctic, for example, icy-cold winds can freeze bare skin in an instant.

Outer layers of clothing must be windproof to keep fast, icy winds from making scientists feel colder.

High-Tech Fabrics

Scientists at the poles cannot simply wear a very thick sweater. Such heavy, bulky clothing makes it hard to work. It also makes people sweat. Sweat is dangerous because, if it freezes on the body, it makes people colder. Instead, scientists wear layered clothing. The layer next to the skin is made of fabric that can wick away sweat. Layers above this are made of lightweight polyester or polypropylene fabric that can trap insulating air between them. The top layer is waterproof, so melting snow and ice do not make the lower layers wet. These layers can be removed and put back on as needed, keeping scientists comfortable.

Avoiding Frostbite

When it is freezing cold, the body diverts blood flow to the main organs to keep them working properly. That means body parts such as the fingers, nose, and toes have less blood flow and can freeze quickly. If left uncovered, these parts can get **frostbite**. Frostbite occurs when cells freeze and die. If untreated, body parts can turn black and need to be amputated (cut off). To avoid frostbite, scientists wear quick-drying fleece material over their head and face, two pairs of warm, waterproof gloves, and insulated boots with an extra waterproof layer over them.

Scientists working outdoors at the poles have to eat about twice as many calories as they would at home.

People can lose up to one-fifth of their body heat from their head, so it is vital to wear a head covering at the poles.

SCIENCE PATROL SURVIVAL

Scientists working out in the field need more food than they do back at the research station. The body has to use a lot more energy to try to keep warm outside. The air is so dry that scientists have to melt ice to make at least 1.8 gallons (8 liters) of water to drink each day if they are to survive.

How do you think dealing with these daily challenges might affect scientists as they work? Give reasons for your answers.

shelter and safety

In order to set up equipment or study weather, wildlife, or ice over a wide area, scientists may have to stay away from the research station for several days or more. They have to take with them not only the scientific equipment needed for their studies, but also somewhere to shelter and rest out of the winds and cold.

Pyramid Tents

Most teams take waterproof, pyramid-shaped tents, which are designed to stay standing in winds of over 60 miles per hour (100 kilometers per hour) and even when a blizzard strikes. Pyramid tents are strong because triangular shapes are more rigid than squares, and do not collapse as easily. By packing snow on top of a skirt of fabric that sticks out around the tent, scientists can ensure it is weighed down and will not blow away. Sometimes people also use tent pegs, rocks, shovels, ice axes, or skis to hold down a tent.

Pyramid tents are usually brightly colored to make them easier to spot in the snow.

Sleeping Soundly

Researchers must stay off the cold ground when they sleep inside a tent. If they do not, they will soon freeze. To sleep, they put a thick rubber sheet over the ground to stop the cold and damp from getting to them, and they sleep on top of an inflatable mattress. The layer of air in the mattress also helps insulate them from the cold. Finally, they sleep on top of a sheepskin and inside a feather-filled sleeping bag.

Navigation and Communication

When people are away from base for several days, the weather can change and bring blizzards or **whiteouts**. Snow piles can shift and change shape, making it even harder for people to know where they are. It is vital to have **navigation equipment**, such as a **global positioning system (GPS)** system that uses **satellites**, to find locations. Communications equipment, such as radios and portable satellite phones, are carried to contact people at the research station, in case of an emergency and to send data back to the labs.

The icy conditions at the poles can sometimes disrupt communications and cut off radio and satellite phone links.

Research Ships

Scientists do not only venture out onto remote areas of ice to do their research. They also explore and undertake scientific research in new areas of the Antarctic and Arctic seas. Trips in polar waters can be dangerous. Drifting icebergs can sink ships and ice-cold water can freeze a person unconscious in minutes.

The strength of the hull on an icebreaker allows it to push deeper into pack ice than other boats.

Icebreakers

Sinking is not the only risk to ships. Pack ice can trap vessels and carry them as the ice drifts for hundreds or thousands of miles before melting, sometimes years later. To travel to remote seas safely, scientists use special ships called icebreakers. Icebreakers have reinforced steel hulls that can crash through thick ice without being damaged. Icebreakers can be over 400 feet (130 meters) long. The larger vessels contain a landing pad for helicopters, cranes to load and unload gear, submarines to collect underwater samples, smaller boats to get into and out of the water, and onboard laboratories.

Working in icy waters is dangerous, so research dinghies carry safety equipment including first aid kits and flares.

Working on an Icebreaker

Icebreakers can survive bumping into an iceberg or other large shards of floating ice found in the Arctic Ocean. Up to 100 scientists and support staff can live and work aboard a fully equipped icebreaker for two months or more.

In the Water

Scientists can leave the main research ship in smaller boats to get among floating ice. If they need to dive into the icy waters, they do not wear wetsuits. Instead they wear neoprene dry suits, which do not allow any water to get inside. They also wear insulating gloves, boots, and head covers. Divers usually stay tethered to a boat and have radio communication with people at the surface while they are below. They carry devices called regulators, through which they get oxygen from scuba tanks. Dry suits often have buttons that inflate and release air to help divers float and sink.

CHAPTER 5

CUTTING-EDGE TECHNOLOGY

Scientists rely on a wide range of technology to collect data about things such as the weather, snow, ice, and what it is like living at the poles. They use machines underwater, on land, and in the air.

Sondes record and transmit data continuously as they rise through the atmosphere.

Weather Records

People's understanding of the climate at the poles is based partly on data from weather stations. These record air pressure, wind speed, precipitation (rain or snow), temperature, and humidity (dampness of air). The instruments automatically record and send data wirelessly to computers, but scientists sometimes have to visit weather stations to maintain them in the freezing temperatures. Scientists locate the stations in the snowy wilderness using GPS. Atmospheric weather data also comes from instruments mounted on sondes, or weather balloons. Sondes can measure the proportions of gases, such as ozone, in the atmosphere. This gas is vital to protect Earth from the sun's harmful **ultraviolet rays** and it is often lowest over Antarctica.

Snow Measurements

The amount of solar energy that the poles reflect is greatest where there is more snow and thicker ice beneath it. On sea ice, the depths of snow and ice can vary greatly, owing to the effect of water movements underneath. Scientists often measure snow thickness using a magnaprobe. Pushing this instrument into the snow measures the depth automatically and sends the data from the exact GPS location wirelessly to a computer. Special electronic instruments measure the thickness of sea ice and also how much water it contains. These instruments can figure out their distance from where ice meets seawater because water **conducts** electricity better than ice. The wetness of ice is important, because wet ice is often weaker and may break up more quickly than drier ice.

Scientists drill holes in the sea ice at Antarctica to check it is deep and safe enough to travel on.

Ice cores

The snow and ice in Antarctica is 1.5 miles (2.5 kilometers) thick. That represents thousands of years of snowfall. It also creates a record of the past atmosphere in the form of bubbles trapped in the snow. Scientists take ice cores to sample the gas in these bubbles. Ice cores are cylinders of ice.

Ice Coring

The ice grows thick as a result of falling snow pressing on the snow beneath, which freezes. This traps not only the water making up the snow, but also tiny air bubbles. Scientists can take short ice cores around 2 inches (51 millimeters) in diameter using electric hand drills. To take deeper, longer samples, they use more powerful drills.

A polar scientist needs to use muscle power to twist the sharp, spiral cutter of a hand auger into the ice.

Double Barrel

The most powerful electric drills scientists use to take ice cores have two barrels around 12 feet (4 meters) long, one spinning inside the other. The inner one has an outer spiral groove and cutters at the end that drill into the ice. The chips of ice the cutters shave away become trapped in the groove. A winch attached to a tower or tripod lowers the drill into the hole it makes. Once the whole drill length is full of ice, spring-loaded teeth snap the ice core away from the ice beneath it. The drill is raised and angled so scientists can get rid of the waste ice and slide out the core onto a tray. The ice is kept frozen while being taken back to the lab for careful testing of the gases in its bubbles.

A scientist bags a length of ice core sample to store and study.

Wide and Deep Cores

Most drills take cores around 4 inches (10 centimeters) in diameter. However, the Blue Ice drill takes cores twice as wide. This enables it to extract far more samples of gas bubbles from the same length of core. The maximum depth of most drills is a quarter mile (400 meters), but the DISC drill can reach depths up to four times this.

ANIMAL STUDIES

Scientists use a wide range of techniques and technologies to find, sample, and count polar animals. They do this to discover where the animals live, how they behave, and their population sizes.

Counting

Scientists use digital cameras to take aerial pictures of polar animals from airplanes and satellites. They can count animals in a group in a photograph by eye, but to do it faster they use computer software. They know where to look for animals based on their understanding of behavior, such as where animals go to feed or breed. In the case of penguin colonies, scientists first scan the landscape for brown patches caused by large amounts of guano (bird droppings).

These are king penguins. Scientists look for penguin droppings to locate a large colony like this.

The tags that scientists stick harmlessly onto whales give a picture of whale journeys across oceans.

Populations of marine animals are usually hidden underwater. Scientists detect underwater animals using echosounders. These machines are attached to boats that send "ping" sounds into the water. The pings echo back when they hit the seabed or animals. On a computer, the pattern of echoes in an area of water shows the size, speed, and depth of any animals. Scientists also use sound to spot and track distant whales. They lower microphones underwater to listen out for whale songs made by particular types of whales.

Tagging is attaching instruments to an animal that send wireless signals about its movements. Scientists may stun animals, such as polar bears, to attach collars with GPS chips. Scientists in boats slowly move close to whales surfacing to breathe, and then attach tags. They use 40-foot (13 meter) poles to push on suction tags, which can stay stuck to the whale for months. The tags provide data about how often the whale moves its tail and rolls as it dives, and how deep and far it swims.

SCIENCE PATROL SURVIVAL

Scientists often have to get near polar animals to study them. The noise of vehicle engines can disturb animals, however. It causes stampedes in walrus herds, for example.

The evidence that scientists collect can help animals, but do you think the positives of their research outweigh the negatives? Should the poles be left free from all interference, even from scientists?

ROBOTS at the POLES

Some of the most cutting-edge technology in use at the poles is found in robots. Robots are machines that can carry out tasks automatically based on computer programming. Using robots avoids the dangers of sending people into freezing waters or beneath thick ice far from the surface.

ROVs

Remote Operated Vehicles, or ROVs, are underwater machines with **propellers** to move around. Cables connected to the ROV and the support boat carry data to and from the robot and supply power to the ROV's equipment. An ROV typically has a video camera and lights at the front, so scientists can see around the robot and what it encounters in the deep waters. It has floats so it does not sink and engines that can twist, enabling the ROV to change direction. ROVs often have tools attached to them, such as tubes to take samples of water and ice and scoops or grabbers to pick up rock samples. One ROV, called SCINI, is narrow enough to drop through small drill holes in an ice shelf. It has many LED lights to take high-quality images of the communities of things that live in the dark and which might change as the ice melts and more sunlight reaches them.

Underwater polar robots help scientists spot the signs of climate change, such as changing ocean temperatures, melting polar ice, and changing populations of ocean life.

On Their Own

Sometimes, even the longest cables are not enough for the distance a robot needs to travel. They might also get tangled as a robot moves around under the ice. Autonomous Underwater Vehicles (AUVs) have their own power supplies and can be operated wirelessly. Some AUVs can explore deep polar waters down to 18,000 feet (5.4 kilometers). Others can travel for hundreds of miles, finding their own routes by detecting sounds from underwater **beacons**. Computers use the signals to control the AUV's speed and direction.

CHAPTER 6

Amazing Discoveries

One of the most significant discoveries scientists have made at the poles is the extent to which polar ice is melting. Understanding the influence of the poles on Earth's climate is vital to understanding how global warming works and how it will impact the poles and the rest of the world.

Effects of the Ice Melt

Using evidence from the poles and other data, scientists have discovered that Earth's temperature has risen more quickly in the past 140 years than at any other time in the past 1,400 years. The ice sheet that covers about 98 percent of Antarctica formed 25 million years ago. It holds about 75 percent of the planet's water in the form of ice.

If the Greenland ice sheet melts, scientists estimate that sea levels would rise about 20 feet (6 meters) and submerge many islands.

Each year Arctic ice melts and reforms. This shows the Arctic sea ice at its annual minimum in September 2012.

Evidence, for example from NASA's space satellite images, shows that Antarctica has been losing more than 24 cubic miles (100 cubic kilometers) of ice each year since 2002. In the Arctic, scientists have found that, over the last 30 years or so, warmer spring temperatures have melted sea ice in the center of the ocean. As ice melts, ocean levels rise. In the last 100 years, average sea levels around the world have risen by 8 inches (20 centimeters) and they are still rising.

This shows the Arctic sea ice at its annual maximum in February 2013.

Other Impacts on the Planet

Scientific discoveries at the poles have also shown how global warming can affect the planet. For example, scientists have discovered that, as well as causing global warming, some of the increased amounts of carbon dioxide in the air are being absorbed by ocean waters. This makes the seawater more **acidic**. Based on their findings, scientists predict that parts of the Southern Ocean will be so acidic in the future that the seawater will start to dissolve the calcium-based shells of sea snails. This will impact polar **food chains** because a host of other animals, including herring, cod, and many whales, eat sea snails. It also tells scientists that more acidic oceans will affect other global structures built from calcium, such as coral reefs.

DISCOVERIES that HELP

Scientists do not just undertake research for themselves. They share the information they gather with other scientists through journals, blogs, and conferences to ensure data are correct and are being interpreted properly. Then, their findings and recommendations help governments and conservation organizations tackle problems such as global warming and find ways to protect the poles.

Making Changes

Scientists' discovery that, if too much ice melts, climate change might speed up and increase sea levels, flooding islands and coastal areas, is inspiring governments to take action. For example, around the world, countries are building more renewable energy plants, erecting

The research that scientists do at the poles is used to inform important conferences about climate change like this one in Paris, France, in 2015.

solar panels to capture the energy of the sun and wind turbines that can use the energy in moving air to generate electricity. Power sources like the sun and wind are called renewable energy because, unlike fossil fuels, they will never run out. More importantly for the poles, they also create fewer polluting greenhouse gases. This should help slow down the rate of global warming.

Aiding Animals

Scientific discoveries help polar animals in practical ways, too. For example, researchers studying penguins, seabirds, and seals in the Southern Ocean around Antarctica identified six "hotspots." Hotspots are areas of marine habitat that are especially important because a large number and range of animals use them for breeding and raising their young. They sometimes occur in areas of open water where animals find a lot of prey to eat. Results like these are important when governments and conservation organizations plan where to establish protected areas in the Southern Ocean. In such areas, human activity is strictly restricted to protect wildlife. Research into wildlife breeding and movement patterns also helps scientists advise organizations about the threats posed to animals If plans for oil drilling in the Arctic are allowed to go ahead in the future.

Installing solar energy systems is one way to reduce greenhouse gas emissions and slow global warming.

PATROLLING the Future

In the future, it is going to be even more important for science patrols to do research at the poles. As ice at the poles melts, there will be new challenges facing the polar regions that could also impact the planet. The discoveries made by scientific patrols today could have a profound impact on everyone's futures.

The Albedo Effect

One vital area of research will be to figure out how much ice is going to melt. The albedo effect, in which white polar ice on land and sea reflects away energy that would be absorbed if it landed elsewhere on Earth's surface, has a cooling effect on the planet. As ice melts, however, the ice that is left is becoming thinner and darker, so it reflects less energy. This makes it more likely to melt and may speed up the rate of melting significantly.

The work scientists are doing at the poles will help protect these precious regions for all of us and for the wildlife that lives there.

As sea ice melts, this opens up wider areas of the ocean to ships and makes it easier for mining and oil companies to reach remote regions to search for resources. Easier access also means more tourist ships will be able to visit the poles. While better access might bring increased awareness of the fragility and importance of the polar regions, it is important that scientists assess what impacts increased human activity could have and what damage even a small oil spill could have.

The latest research stations rely on new technology and new design ideas to help them cope with the challenging conditions at the poles.

SCIENCE PATROL SURVIVAL

In Antarctica, there are more than 60 scientific bases belonging to 27 different countries. In summer, more than 4,000 scientists are in the region conducting experiments. They need somewhere to live, relax, and work. Imagine you are going to design your own research station. These questions might help you figure out what to include:

- *What recreation facilities would you include?*
- *How many labs would you build and which labs would have the largest space?*
- *Will it be a floating station on Arctic ice or a permanent one on the Antarctic coast?*
- *What vehicles will you include for scientists to use when exploring the ice and oceans beyond the station?*
- *Will you include an aquarium?*
- *What about places for ships to dock and planes to land?*

Glossary

acidic containing acids, substances that are very strong and can damage surfaces

adapted having features that make something suitable to a life in a particular habitat

antifreeze a substance used to lower the freezing point of water

atmosphere a blanket of gases around a planet

bacteria tiny, living things

barren describes land without any plant life

beacons devices that can send out radio signals (or light)

blizzards snowstorms

breeding having young or babies

calories units of measurement for the amount of energy in a particular food

carbon dioxide a gas in the atmosphere that is linked to global warming

climate the usual pattern of weather that happens in a place

climate change changes in the world's weather patterns caused by human activity

conducts transmits or passes on

conservation the protection of animals, plants, and natural resources

data facts and statistics

dehydrated when something has the water removed from it

distemper a disease that causes fever and coughing in animals

endangered in danger of dying out and becoming extinct

environment the natural world in which plants and animals live

food chains sequences of plants and animals that are linked together because each one eats or is eaten by another

frostbite damage caused to parts of the body, such as fingers, when they freeze

glaciers large, very slow-moving masses of ice

Global Positioning System (GPS) a system that uses signals from satellites in space to locate positions on Earth

greenhouse gases gases that trap heat in the atmosphere

habitat a place in nature where animals live

hulls the bodies of boats or ships

hypothermia a condition in which the body becomes too cold to work properly

ice sheets masses of glacier ice that cover a large area of land

icebergs huge chunks of ice formed from fresh water that floats in polar oceans

incinerator a machine for burning waste

insulating describes something that reduces or prevents the flow of heat

meteorology the study of weather

navigation equipment devices used to find one's way around

pack ice a mass of ice floating on the sea

plankton tiny animal and plant life in an ocean

pollute to spoil, make dirty, or even poison the air, soil, or water

predators animals that catch other animals for food

propellers parts with two or more blades that turn quickly to make a ship or airplane move

reflects bounces back

renewable something that can be replaced

satellites electronic devices high in space that move around Earth

snow blindness temporary blindness caused by light reflecting off snow

solar power electricity made from sunlight

species a type of plant or animal

tundra a large area of flat land where there are no trees and the ground is always frozen

ultraviolet rays invisible beams of light within sunlight that can damage skin

whiteouts types of snowstorm in which blowing or falling snow and clouds make it very difficult to see

wind turbines machines that capture the wind's energy to make electricity

For more information

Books

DK Adventures: *Antarctic Expedition*. New York, NY: DK Publishing, 2015.

Mahoney, Emily. *Antarctic Researchers* (Out of the Lab: Extreme Jobs in Science). New York, NY: PowerKids Press, 2016.

Petersen, Christine. *Learning about Antarctica* (Searchlight Books Do You Know the Continents?). Minneapolis, MN: Lerner Classroom, 2015.

Websites

Discover more about global warming and the Arctic region at:
www.climatekids.nasa.gov/arctic-animals

Watch a video about Antarctica at:
**www.video.nationalgeographic.com/video/destinations/
antarctica-overview-dest**

The United States Antarctic Research Program website has a lot of information at:
www.usap.gov/usapgov/aboutTheContinent/index.cfm?m=2

Publisher's note to educators and parents: Our editors have carefully reviewed these websites to ensure that they are suitable for students. Many websites change frequently, however, and we cannot guarantee that a site's future contents will continue to meet our high standards of quality and educational value. Be advised that students should be closely supervised whenever they access the Internet.

index

adaptations 11
albedo efffect 44
Amundsen-Scott South Pole Station 23
Antarctic cod 23
Antarctic Treaty 13
Antarctica 4, 5, 11, 13, 14, 16, 17, 32, 33, 34, 40, 41, 43, 45
Arctic 4, 5, 11, 12, 17, 21, 30, 41, 43, 45
Arctic cod 11
Arctic hares 8
Arctic Ocean 5, 12, 15, 17, 31
Arctic willow 11
Arctic wolves 8
atmosphere 14, 15, 22, 32, 34
Autonomous Underwater Vehicles (AUVs) 39

birds 12, 13, 21, 36, 43

Canada 5
carbon dioxide 15, 22, 41
climate 6, 14, 15, 32, 40
climate change 14–15, 39, 42
clothing 21, 26
conservation 23, 42, 43
coral reefs 41

data 6, 16, 24, 29, 32, 33, 37, 38, 40, 42
dog sleds 24

Finland 5
fish 10, 12, 13
fishing 13
food 13, 14, 18–19, 21, 27
food chains 41
France 42
frostbite 27
fuels 21, 22, 43

glaciers 4
Global Positioning System (GPS) 29, 32, 33, 37

global warming 14, 15, 40, 41, 42, 43
greenhouse gases 15, 43
Greenland 5, 40

Halley VI 17
hypothermia 6, 18

ice 4, 5, 6, 7, 8, 9, 11, 12, 13, 14, 15, 17, 21, 23, 24, 25, 26, 27, 28, 30, 31, 32, 33, 34–35, 38, 39, 40, 41, 42, 44, 45
icebergs 11, 30, 31
icebreakers 30, 31
Iceland 5

krill 10, 13, 23

lemmings 8
leopard seals 9, 10

McMurdo 16, 20, 21, 23
meteorites 11
meteorology 23

North Pole 4, 5, 17
Norway 5

oil 12, 13, 43, 45
orcas 10

Patagonian toothfish 13
penguins 10, 11, 36, 43
plankton 10
plants 4, 5, 10, 11, 18, 19, 21, 42
polar bears 8, 9, 10, 37
pollution 20, 21, 22
predators 9, 10, 21

reindeer 8
Remote Operated Vehicles (ROVs) 38
research 13, 17, 23, 24, 30, 37, 42, 43, 44

research ships 30–31
research stations 16, 17, 18, 19, 20, 21, 22, 23, 24, 27, 28, 29, 45
Russia 5

samples 6, 12, 30, 34, 35, 36, 38
satellites 29, 36, 41
Scott, Robert Falcon 9
sea levels 15, 40, 41, 42
sea lions 10
sea snails 23, 41
sea spiders 23
Sno-Cats 24, 25
snow 4, 6, 7, 8, 11, 17, 18, 21, 24, 25, 26, 28, 29, 32, 33, 34
snow blindness 7
snowmobiles 24
sondes 32
South Pole 4, 6, 7, 9, 23
Southern Ocean 41, 43
sponges 23
starfish 23
summer 4, 5, 6, 7, 15, 16, 45
Sweden 5

tagging 37
tardigrades 10, 11
tents 28, 29
tundra 4, 5, 8

United States 5
urchins 23

walruses 9, 11, 14, 15, 37
waste disposal 20
weather balloons 32
weather stations 32
whales 9, 10, 11, 37, 41
whiteouts 29
wind turbines 22, 43
winds 4, 8, 11, 22, 26, 28, 32, 43
winter 4, 5, 6, 7, 16